The Lessons of John G. Lake

on

Prayer

The Lessons of John G. Lake on

Prayer

LARRY KEEFAUVER,
GENERAL EDITOR

CREATION
HOUSE
Orlando, FL

THE LESSONS OF JOHN G. LAKE ON PRAYER
A Charisma Classics Bible Study
Larry Keefauver, General Editor
Published by Creation House
Strang Communications Company
600 Rinehart Road
Lake Mary, Florida 32746
Web site: http://www.creationhouse.com

Contents

Introduction

WELCOME TO this devotional study guide on *The Lessons of John G. Lake on Prayer*. This study is a companion volume to *The Original John G. Lake Devotional*.

This devotional study is part of a series of four Bible study guides focused on the teachings of some of the founding leaders of the Spirit-filled, Pentecostal movement—Smith Wigglesworth, John G. Lake, Maria Woodworth-Etter, and William J. Seymour from Azusa Street. Do not feel that you must go through this series in any particular order. Choose the guide and sequence that best meet your spiritual needs.

John Graham Lake's life began with the need for a healing miracle. Born in 1870 in Ontario, Canada, one of sixteen children, John Lake struggled as a child with a digestive disease that almost robbed him of life. While he did survive, eight of his brothers and sisters died. From the outset, John Lake knew that sickness and sorrow were evil attacks that only the power of God could ultimately overcome.

Lake's family moved to Michigan when he was sixteen. While there, John Lake was saved in a Salvation Army meeting and joined a Methodist church. He sought God, desperately desiring to learn how to break the curse of disease and death off his family. At church, the pastor and members told him to endure patiently while he watched his body become deformed by crippling rheumatism.

Deep down inside, John Lake knew that sickness was not God's will for his life—or for anyone else's, for that matter. He sought God's healing at John Alexander Dowie's Divine Healing Home in Chicago. While there God's power surged through his weak and deformed body, completely straightening his limbs and healing him. John Lake had encountered what he later termed "a strong man's gospel."

Though his earlier education had focused on engineering, at age twenty-one Lake redirected his studies to become a Methodist minister. In 1891 he married Jennie Stevens. They had seven children.

Five years after their wedding, the Lakes discovered that Jennie had tuberculosis and incurable heart disease. Lake found himself surrounded by affliction and attacks of the enemy—two of his sisters were critically ill, his brother was an invalid, and his beloved wife weakened daily.

Once again John Lake sought God's power and contacted Dowie in Chicago, asking for his prayers. In the coming months both of his sisters were healed, but his dear Jennie remained deathly ill. John Lake and his wife held onto God all the more and claimed Acts 10:38, "God anointed Jesus of Nazareth with the Holy Ghost and with power: who went about doing good, and healing all that were oppressed of the devil; for God was with him."

Lake understood that the source of disease was an attack of the devil and that Jesus was with them through the power of the Holy Spirit. He came to believe that the same power of the Holy Spirit was also in him by faith in Christ through the indwelling Holy Spirit. So he called his friends and announced that at 9:30 A.M. on April 28, 1898, Jennie would be healed. At the appointed time, Lake laid his hands on his wife and immediately her paralysis left, her heart began beating normally, her breathing and temperature returned to normal, and she declared, "Praise God! I am healed!"

John Lake and his family now knew God's healing power as a reality for themselves and others. After a few years of working very successfully in business, amassing a small fortune while ministering part time, John Lake continued to cry out for more of God. For nine months in 1907, Lake fasted and prayed for the baptism of the Holy Spirit. Suddenly the baptism fell, and Lake was filled to overflowing with God's Spirit. He became so sensitized to the Spirit that he could lay hands on people and reveal to them their illnesses before they ever spoke.

Lake left business and entered into a full-time evangelistic healing ministry. God led him and fellow workers to South Africa, where thousands were reached over the years for Christ, and scores were healed by the power of God. He established a main church in Johannesburg and planted over one hundred churches in surrounding areas. His staff grew to more than a hundred and twenty-five ministers. But in the midst of great advances, there were many financial difficulties, and not even a year into his ministry, his beloved Jennie died while he was in Africa.

Undaunted, Lake returned to America to care for his children and to raise funds for the work in South Africa. He founded the Apostolic Faith Mission and the Zion Christian Church, which grew to over six hundred congregations with a hundred thousand converts, and witnessed countless miracles by 1913.

By the end of 1913, Lake moved to Spokane, Washington. There he started a healing clinic and began training healing technicians to minister God's power to the sick.

The International Apostolic Congress, headquartered in Spokane, continued to grow worldwide under Lake's leadership. In 1920, Lake moved to Portland, Oregon, to oversee another Apostolic church. By 1924, newspapers reported John Lake as a nationally known healing evangelist with forty churches in the United States and Canada. It was also reported that Spokane, Washington, had experienced over a hundred thousand healings through Lake's ministry and was the healthiest place in America to reside.

His endless travels, crusades, church plantings, and healing clinics drained his physical strength. Still filled with vision, bold faith, and a strong man's gospel, John Lake met the Healer face to face in September 1935.

This devotional study guide may be used by individuals, groups, or classes. A leader's guide for group or class sessions is provided at the end of this devotional study for those using this guide in a group setting. Groups using this guide should complete their devotional studies prior to their group sessions. This will greatly enhance sharing, studying and praying together.

Individuals going through this guide can use it for daily devotional reading and study. The purpose of this guide is to help the reader(s) understand prayer through the Scriptures with the insights of John G. Lake. All of the insights quoted from Lake's precise words are placed between lines and italicized for easy recognition. Each daily devotional study is structured to:

❖ Probe deeply into the Scriptures.
❖ Examine your personal relationship in faith with Jesus Christ and your prayer life.
❖ Discover biblical truths about prayer.
❖ Encounter Jesus Christ as personal Lord and Savior.

It is our prayer that as you study about prayer daily in this devotional study, you will be empowered by the Holy Spirit to trust Jesus Christ in every aspect of your life.

Day 1

Believe When You Pray

When ye pray, believe that ye receive them, and ye shall have them.

—MARK 11:24

GOD IS NOT *the God of the dead. He is the God of the living. The desire in my soul is that in this nation God Almighty may raise up an altar unto the living God, not unto a dead God. Humanity needs an altar to the living God, to the God that hears prayer, to the God that answers prayer, and to the God that answers by fire. God is saying, "If there is a Christian, let him pray. If there is a God, let Him answer."*

When and how often do you pray believing that you will receive? Put an *x* on the line to indicate where you are right now:

I pray . . .

Often	Sometimes	Never

Believing to receive	Doubting

Just talking	Talking and listening	Listening

Silently	Aloud

My own words	My words and His	The Word
In my mind		In the Spirit
For my needs		For others
Habitually		Spontaneously

IN EMPHASIZING THIS, *the Lord Jesus Christ says to the world, "When ye pray, believe that ye receive them, and ye shall have them" (Mark 11:24). That is what is the matter. Your blank check is not worth ten cents in your hands. Why? Because you do not believe God. Fill in your check, believe God, and it will come to pass.*

Praying in faith is rooted in the promises of God. All of God's promises can be trusted, because He is faithful. Read each of the following passages, and write down what is revealed about the promises of God.

Psalm 105:42 _____

_____

Luke 1:54 _____

_____

2 Corinthians 1:20 _____

_____

Titus 1:2 _____

_____

Hebrews 10:23 _____

_____

    Praying in faith does not depend on your strength but His; not your efforts but His grace; and not your will but His will. Pray in His name and will, trusting Him—not yourself—and your prayers will be answered. The three most common answers from God to our prayers are: *Yes, No,* or *Wait.* Complete these sentences:

When God says *Yes,* my response is usually _____

_____.

When God says *No,* my response is usually _____

_____.

When God says *Wait,* my response is usually _____

_____.

    When you pray, pray *believing* that God will answer in His will, with His best, and in His timing.

Ask Yourself . . .

❖ Do you pray believing God will answer?
❖ Do you pray trusting God or trusting yourself to manipulate God?
❖ Do you pray the Word of God?

Write a prayer asking in faith for what you need:

_____

_____

_____

Day 2

The Soul Cry of Prayer

For they had sworn with all their heart, and sought him [God] with their whole desire; and he was found of them.

—2 CHRONICLES 15:15

WE ARE SOMETIMES *inclined to think of God as mechanical; as though God set a date for this event or that to occur. But my opinion is that one of the works of the Holy Ghost is that of preparer. He comes and prepares the heart of His people in advance by putting a strange hunger for that event that has been promised by God until it comes to pass. The more I study history and prophecy, the more I am convinced that when Jesus Christ was born into the world, He was born in answer to a tremendous heart cry on the part of the world.*

Prayer prepares our hearts to receive what God has for us. Below are the different parts of the Lord's prayer. Rewrite each phrase in your own words:

Our Father, which art in heaven,

_____

Hallowed be Thy name.

_____

Thy kingdom come. Thy will be done in earth, as it is in heaven.

Give us this day our daily bread.

And forgive us our debts, as we forgive our debtors.

And lead us not into temptation, but deliver us from evil:

For thine is the kingdom, and the power, and the glory, for ever. Amen.

When you pray, how does God prepare your heart for His Word and His will?

GOD'S PURPOSES COME *to pass when your heart, and mine, get the real God-cry, and the real God-prayer comes into our spirit, and the real God-yearning gets hold of our nature. Something is going to happen then.*

When your heart cries out to God, how do you pray? Check all that apply to you:

- ❏ I weep before the Lord.
- ❏ I pray in the Spirit or tongues.
- ❏ I rejoice before the Lord.
- ❏ I pray with groanings in the Spirit.

❏ I sing a new song to the Lord.
❏ I silently listen, being still before the Lord.
❏ Other: _____

Ask Yourself . . .

❖ Are you changed in the Lord's presence when you pray?
❖ How does God prepare your heart when you pray?

Write a prayer asking God to prepare your heart for His purposes as you seek His presence:

_____

_____

_____

Day 3

Praying With Conviction

The effectual fervent prayer of a righteous man availeth much.

—JAMES 5:16

NE DAY Don Von Vuuren received a letter from friends in Johannesburg telling of the coming of what they spoke of as "the American brethren," and of the wonderful things that were taking place. Of how So-and-so, a terrible drunkard, had been converted. Of how his niece who had been an invalid in a wheelchair for five years had been healed of God, and how one of his other relatives had been baptized in the Holy Ghost and was speaking in tongues. And of all the marvels a vigorous work for God produces.

Don Von Vuuren took the letter and crawled under an African thorn tree. He spread the letter out before God, and began to discuss it with the Lord. He said, "God in heaven, if You could come to Mr. So-and-so, a drunkard, and deliver him from his sin and save his soul and put the joy of God in him; if You could come to this niece of mine, save her soul and heal her body and send her out to be a blessing instead of a weight and burden upon her friends; and if You could come to So-and-so and he was baptized in the Holy Ghost and spoke in tongues, then Lord, You can do something for me too." So he knelt down, put his face to the ground, and cried to God.

And God came down into his life. In ten minutes he took all the breath he wanted; the pain was gone, his tuberculosis had disappeared, he was a whole man.

For what are you crying out to God? Check all that apply to you:

- ❏ Healing
- ❏ Financial prosperity
- ❏ To be saved
- ❏ To be baptized by the Holy Spirit
- ❏ For the needs of someone else
- ❏ For your family
- ❏ For your marriage
- ❏ Other: _____

God will answer your prayer. James declares that the effectual, fervent prayer of the righteous avails much. If you are praying and not receiving an answer, do a righteousness check of your life. Read these verses, and then list how you receive righteousness:

1 Corinthians 1:26–31 _____

_____

Romans 5:6–11 _____

_____

Romans 5:18–21 _____

_____

Romans 3:23–26 _____

_____

Faith in Christ imparts His righteousness to us. Therefore pray in faith trusting Him for your righteousness. Pray this prayer: *Jesus, forgive me of my sins. Make me righteous through Your shed blood. Answer my prayer through Jesus. Amen.*

Day 3

Ask Yourself . . .

❖ Are you praying by faith?
❖ Have you received the righteousness of Christ?

Write a prayer seeking His righteousness and His presence, since all you need is in Christ:

_____

_____

_____

Day 4

Seek With Faith and Prayer

And all things, whatsoever ye shall ask in prayer, believing, ye shall receive.

—MATTHEW 21:22

WILLIAM SEYMOUR TOLD me, "Brother, before I met Parham, such a hunger to have more of God was in my heart that I prayed for five hours a day for two-and-a-half years. I got to Los Angeles, and when I got there the hunger was not less but more. I prayed, 'God, what can I do?' And the Spirit said, 'Pray more.' 'But Lord, I am praying five hours a day now.' I increased my hours of prayer to seven, and prayed on for a year-and-a-half more. I prayed, 'God, give me what Parham preached, the real Holy Ghost and fire, with tongues and love and power of God like the apostles had.'"

Are you ready to receive what those early Christians received at Pentecost? Read the first two chapters of Acts, and then complete these sentences:

Jesus promised _____

_____.

Jesus commanded them to_____

_____.

In obedience, they _____

_____.

Day 4

When the Holy Spirit fell on them, they experienced

_____ .

I desire with my heart to _____

_____ .

HERE ARE BETTER *things to be had in spiritual life but they must be sought out with faith and prayer. I want to tell you, God Almighty had put such a hunger into Seymour's heart that when the fire of God came it glorified him.*

I wonder what we are hungering for? Have we a real divine hunger, something our soul is asking for? If we have, God will answer, God will answer. By every law of the Spirit that men know, the answer is due to come. It will come! Bless God, it will come. It will come in more ways than we ever dreamed.

Have you experienced in your spiritual life what the early Christians experienced? Listed below are some of the characteristics of their experiences. Circle all that you have encountered in your life, and underline those that you hunger for:

Speaking in unknown tongues

Filled with the Holy Spirit

Operating in the power of the Spirit

Praying in the Spirit

Boldly witnessing for Christ

Miracles

Healings

Deliverance

Joyful giving unto the Lord

Hunger for the Word of God

Love and unity with other believers

Ask Yourself . . .

❖ What do you hunger for from the Holy Spirit?
❖ How is the power of the Holy Spirit being manifested in your life?

Write a prayer, asking God's Spirit for a deep hunger for all that He has for you:

_____

_____

_____

Day 5

Praying From the Heart

*A new heart also will I give you, and a new spirit will
I put within you: and I will take away the stony heart
out of your flesh, and I will give you a heart of flesh.*
— EZEKIEL 36:26

THERE IS PROBABLY *no more delightful thing on earth than to
watch a soul praying to God, when the light of God comes on
and the life of God fills the nature, and that holy affection that
we seek from others finds expression in Him. That is what the Lord is
asking from you; and if you want to gratify the heart of Jesus Christ,
that is the only way in all the world to do it.*

The light that comes on when a believer prays to God is
the baptism by fire that only the Holy Spirit brings. That
fire purges and burns aways all unholiness and sin while
purifying the believer. The light of Christ reveals every sin,
and the Spirit's convicting fire burns it away.

Read the following verses and then write down below
all that the Spirit needs to burn away in your life
(Isa. 32:14–16; Matt. 3:11–12; 2 Cor. 7:1; Gal. 5:16–26;
Heb. 12:29):

_____

_____

_____

HE INVITATION FROM *Christ is not, "Give Me thine head." The invitation is, "My son, give Me thine heart." That is an affectionate relationship, a real love union in God.*

The Lord desires that you love Him with your whole heart. He will settle for nothing less than your full heart's devotion and passion for Him.

In the heart pictured below, shade in to the level of your present love for Him.

Now discover what the Lord desires to do with your heart. Read the passages below and write down how your heart needs to respond to the Lord:

Psalm 28:7 _____

_____

Psalm 51:10–17 _____

_____

Psalm 119:11 _____

_____

Day 5

Proverbs 4:23 _____

_____

Ezekiel 18:31, 36:26 _____

_____

Matthew 22:37 _____

_____

John 7:38 _____

_____

Ask Yourself . . .

❖ Is your heart totally committed and in love with the Lord?
❖ Are you praying from your heart or just your mind?

Write a heart prayer expressing your love for Christ:

_____

_____

_____

Day 6

The Prayer of Faith

The prayer of faith shall save the sick, and the Lord shall raise him up.

—JAMES 5:15

T HE PRAYER OF *faith has power. The prayer of faith has trust. The prayer of faith has healing for soul and body. The disciples wanted to know how to pray real prayers, and Jesus said unto them, "When ye pray, say, Our Father which art in heaven . . . Thy will be done"* (Luke 11:2).

How do you pray for the sick? Write down a prayer using the usual ways that you pray for someone who is sick:

_____

_____

_____

Now examine your prayer. Circle all the words below that describe the prayer you have just written.

Bold	Passive
In faith	Doubtful
Assured	Unsure
Knowing God's will	Not knowing
Confident	Fearful
Hopeful	Hopeless
Joyful	Depressed

If you circled more words on the right column than on the left, then your prayer may lack the faith and power to trust God for healing.

VERYBODY STOPS THERE—at "Thy will be done."—and they resign their intelligence at that point to the unknown God.
When you approach people and say to them, "You have missed the spirit of prayer," they look at you in amazement. But, beloved, it is a fact I want to show to you, as it is written in the Word of God. It does not say, "If it be thy will," and stop there. There is a comma there, not a period. The prayer is this, "Thy will be done, as in heaven, so in earth" (Luke 11:2).
That is a mite different, is it not? Not, "Thy will be done. Let the calamity come. Let my children be stricken with fever, or my son go to the insane asylum, or my daughter go to the home of the feeble-minded." That is not what Jesus was teaching the people to pray. Jesus was teaching the people to pray, "Thy will be done on earth as it is in heaven." Let the might of God be known. Let the power of God descend. Let God avert the calamity that is coming. Let it turn aside through faith in God. "Thy will be done on earth as it is in heaven."

God's will is that people be healed and in good health. Read these passages, and write down what they declare about God's will for healing:

Exodus 15:26 _____

Psalm 107:20 _____

Psalm 103:1–5 _____

Isaiah 53:5 _____

_____

Jeremiah 17:14 _____

_____

Luke 4:18 _____

_____

Mark 16:18 _____

_____

James 5:14–15 _____

_____

3 John 2 _____

_____

Ask Yourself . . .

❖ Do you truly believe it is God's will to heal?
❖ Do you trust Him completely to heal in His way and His timing?

Read again how you pray for the sick, and now rewrite your prayer in faith, knowing that it is God's will to heal:

_____

_____

_____

Day 7

Believing, Pray for Healing

When ye pray, believe that ye receive them, and ye shall have them.

—MARK 11:24

HERE IS NO *question in the mind of God concerning the salvation of a sinner. No more is there question concerning the healing of the sick one. It is in the atonement of Jesus Christ, bless God. His atonement was unto the uttermost; to the last need of man.*

Remember, God's healing does not rest in the power of your faith but in the power of His faithfulness. He does not ask you to trust your praying but to trust Him, who answers your prayers. What keeps you from trusting Him for healing?

Check all that apply.

❏ Past experience
❏ Pain
❏ Hurt
❏ Fear
❏ Unbelief
❏ Ignorance of the Word
❏ Other: _____

HE RESPONSIBILITY *rests purely, solely, and entirely on man. Jesus put it there. Jesus said, "When ye pray, believe that ye receive them, and ye shall have them." No questions, or ifs, in the words of Jesus. If He ever spoke with emphasis on any question, it was on the subject of God's will and the result of faith in prayer. Indeed, He did not even speak them in ordinary words, but in the custom of the East. He said, "Verily, verily." Amen, amen — the same as if I were to stand in an American court and say, "I swear to tell the truth, the whole truth, and nothing but the truth, so help me God."*

So instead of praying, "Lord, if it be Thy will" when you kneel beside your sick friend, Jesus Christ has commanded you, and every believer, to lay your hands on the sick. This is not my ministry nor my brethren's only. It is the ministry of every believer. And if your ministers do not believe it, God have mercy on them. If your churches do not believe it, God have mercy on them.

The responsibility to pray for the healing of others rests entirely on us. Consider this: *What if God's healing is not released in another's life because we did not pray?* How many could be healed if you prayed? How many are not being healed because of your prayerlessness?

Right now make a list of all those who you know who need healing—physical, emotional, or relational.

Name   **Healing Needed**

_____   _____
_____   _____
_____   _____
_____   _____
_____   _____

Day 7

Ask Yourself . . .

- ❖ Are you willing to pray for those who need healing?
- ❖ Will you repent of not praying for the healing of others?

Write a prayer for the healing of another person:

_____

_____

_____

Day 8

In His Name

Whatsoever ye shall ask the Father in my name, he will give it you.

—JOHN 16:23

MATCHLESS NAME! *The secret of power was in it. When the disciples used the name the power struck. The dynamite of heaven exploded. Peter and John were hustled off to jail. The church prayed for them "in the name." They were released. They went to the church.*

The entire church prayed that signs and wonders might be done. How did they pray? In "the name." They used it legally. The vital response was instantaneous. The place was shaken as by an earthquake. Tremendous name!

What power is in His name! Read these scriptures and then write down what they reveal about the power of the name of Jesus (Matt. 18:20; Mark 9:39; Luke 9:48; John 5:43, 14:13, 16:16, 16:23–26; Acts 3:16, 4:12, Eph. 1:21; Col. 3:17).

Jesus

Day 8

ESUS COMMANDED: *"Go into all the world."* Why? To proclaim
the name. To use the name. In it was concentrated the combined
authority resident in the Father, the Son, and the Holy Ghost.

The apostles used the name. It worked. The deacons at Samaria
used the name. The fire flashed. Believers everywhere, forever, were
commanded to use it. The name detonated around the world.

Prayer in His name gets answers. The Moravians prayed. The
greatest revival till that time hit the world. Finney prayed. America
rocked with power. Hudson Taylor prayed. China's Inland Mission
was born. Evan Roberts prayed seven years. The Welsh revival
resulted. Pray in the name of Jesus!

When we pray in the name of Jesus, we are praying in
His will, power, and authority. Nothing happens when
we pray in any other name but His!

Make a list of all the people and things you need to
pray about in His name:

_____

_____

_____

_____

_____

_____

Ask Yourself . . .

❖ Are you praying in the authority and power of His name?

❖ What hinders you from praying in His name?

Write a prayer of authority and power in His name for the most important need in your life:

_____

_____

_____

Day 9

A Prayer for the Inner Life

For this cause I bow my knees unto the Father of our Lord Jesus Christ . . . that he would grant you . . . to be strengthened with might by his Spirit in the inner man.
—EPHESIANS 3:14, 16

MY GOD, *we bless Thee for the ideal of the gospel of Christ which Thou hast established in the souls of men through the blessed Holy Ghost. God, we pray Thee this afternoon that if we have thought lightly of the Spirit of God, if we have had our eyes fixed on outward evidences instead of the inward life, we pray Thee to sweep it away from our souls.*

May we this day, God, see indeed that the life of God—His Life in our inner selves revealed by Christ's perfect life—is to be revealed in us. May the Lord Jesus through us shed forth His glory, life, benediction, peace, and power upon the world. Blessed be Thy precious Name.

Pray for your inner life. Pray for your life of prayer and deep communion with the Father. One way to pray effectively is to pray the Word.

Below is a prayer adapted from Ephesians 3:16–21. Pray it aloud, and put your name in the blanks:

A Prayer for My Inner Life

    Lord Jesus, grant that _____*, according to the riches of Your glory, might be strengthened with might by Your Spirit in* _____*'s inner man; that Christ may dwell in* _____*'s heart by faith; that* _____*, being rooted and grounded in love, may be able to comprehend, with all saints, what is the breadth, and length, and depth, and height, and for* _____ *to know the love of Christ, which passeth knowledge, that* _____ *might be filled with all the fullness of God.*

    Now unto him who is able to do exceedingly abundantly above all that _____ *can ask or think, according to the power that worketh in* _____*, unto him be glory in the church by Christ Jesus throughout all ages, world without end. Amen.*

    So my God, we open our nature to heaven today, asking that the Spirit of the living God will thus move in our own soul, that by His grace we shall be so perfectly, truly cleansed of God that our nature will be sweet, pure, heavenly, and true.

    We desire to receive from God the blessed sweetness of His pure, holy, heavenly Spirit to reign in us, to rule over us, to control us, and to guide us forevermore. Amen.

    Read the prayer written above. Underline the part that speaks most to your inner man. Then pray the prayer aloud, substituting "I" for "we," "my" for "our," and "me" for "us."

Ask Yourself . . .

❖ Are you praying for your inner life with Christ?
❖ How is He strengthening your inner man?

Write a prayer thanking Christ for doing exceedingly more than you could ever ask or think:

_____

_____

_____

Day 10

Before Prayer—Overcome Pride

Let this mind be in you, which was also in Christ Jesus: Who, being in the form of God . . . humbled himself, and became obedient unto death.
—PHILIPPIANS 2:5–6, 8

AT HIS LAST SUPPER *with the disciples, knowing that all power had been given unto Him, Jesus took a towel and a basin and proceeded to wash the disciples' feet. When He had finished He said, "Know ye what I have done to you?" (John 13:12). In explanation He said, "If I then, your Lord and Master, have washed your feet; ye also ought to wash one another's feet" (John 13:14).*

Authentic prayer requires humility. Read the parable of the Pharisee and the publican (tax collector) in Luke 18:9–14, and then complete these sentences:

The Pharisee prayed _____ .

The tax collector prayed _____ .

God responded to _____ .

WHEN WE EXAMINE *the human heart and endeavor to discover what it is that retards our progress, I believe we will find that pride in the human soul is perhaps the greatest difficulty we have to overcome. Jesus taught us a wonderful humility, taking the place of a servant. We are enjoined to thus treat and love one another. His presence with us, His presence in us must produce in our hearts the same conditions that were in His own. It must bring into our life the same humility that was in Him. It is one of the secrets of entrance into the grace of God.*

Read Philippians 2:5–8 and Galatians 2:20. What elements of your selfish pride need to be crucified? On the cross below, write what needs to be crucified in you:

Ask Yourself . . .

❖ Has your pride been crucified?
❖ Do you crucify self daily on the cross?

Write a prayer confessing any pride that you need to repent of to Christ:

Day 11

Intercession

Blessed are they that mourn: for they shall be comforted.

—MATTHEW 5:4

THIS FIGURE IS *taken from the old prophets, who, when the nation sinned, took upon themselves the responsibility of the nation. They put sackcloth on their bodies, and ashes on their heads, and in mourning and tears went down before God for days and weeks until the people turned to God. They became the intercessors between God and man.*

Moses became the great intercessor. When God said to him, after the Israelites had made the golden calf, "Let me alone ... that I may consume them: and I will make of thee a great nation" (Exod. 32:10), Moses said, "Wherefore should the Egyptians speak, and say, For mischief did he bring them out, to slay them in the mountains, and to consume them from the face of the earth?" (v. 12). God had said to Moses, "I will make of thee a great nation;" but Moses was big enough to turn aside the greatest honor that God could bestow upon a man, that of becoming the father of a race. He pleaded with God, "Oh, this people have sinned a great sin, and have made them gods of gold. Yet now, if thou wilt forgive their sin —; and if not, blot me, I pray thee, out of thy book" (Exod. 32:31–32).

Intercession is not us laying the burdens of our hearts on God, but rather being open for God to burden our hearts to pray for what He desires. List three people and what God has laid on your heart to intercede for in their lives. Then pray for them:

God desires me to pray for: Concerning . . .

_____	_____
_____	_____
_____	_____
_____	_____
_____	

$\mathfrak{B}$ LESSED IS THE *intercessor who comprehends the purposes of God, who understands his responsibility and possibility, who by God-given mourning and crying turns the people to God. With a heart yearning for sinners, an intercessor becomes a mourner before God, and takes upon himself the responsibility of fallen sinners. He goes down in tears and repentance before God, until people turn to God and mercy is shown to them.*

Are you willing to intercede for the sins of others and of the nation?

Read 2 Chronicles 7:14. Write a prayer of intercession for the sins of your nation:

_____

_____

_____

Read Daniel 9:3–11. Write a prayer of intercession for the people of God, the church:

_____

_____

_____

Ask Yourself . . .

❖ Are you willing to intercede daily for the sins of others?

❖ Will you allow God to place His intercession in your heart for others?

Spend time in prayer now, interceding for the sins of your family, your church, and your community.

_____

_____

_____

Day 12

Changed by the Spirit

But we all, with open face beholding as in a glass the glory of the Lord, are changed into the same image from glory to glory, even as by the Spirit of the Lord.
—2 CORINTHIANS 3:18

HOW BEAUTIFUL IT *is to have the privilege of looking into the face of one whose nature has been thus refined by the Spirit of the living God within. How beautiful it is when we look into the soul of one who has been purged by the blood of Christ until the very characteristics of the life and attitudes of the mind of Christ are manifest.*

Prayer brings us into the presence of the Spirit. In His presence, we are changed. Describe one way the Spirit has been changing you as you pray:

_____

_____

CHRISTIANITY IS A *strong man's gospel. Christianity, by the grace of God, is calculated to take the weak, fallen, erring, suffering, and dying, and to apply the grace and power of God, through the soul of man, to the need of the individual.*

Christ makes us strong. We are not strong in our own strength or efforts, but by His grace we receive His power to do His will. Read the following passages, and write down how you become strong through God's grace in Christ:

Psalm 23 _____

_____

Psalm 27:1 _____

_____

Ecclesiastes 7:19 _____

_____

Zechariah 4:6 _____

_____

2 Corinthians 12:9–19 _____

_____

Ephesians 4:16–20 _____

_____

Philippians 4:13, 19 _____

_____

1 John 4:4 _____

_____

Day 12

Ask Yourself . . .

❖ Are you relying on His strength or your own?
❖ How are you being His strong person today?

Write a prayer confessing your own weaknesses and seeking His strength:

_____

_____

_____

Day 13

Being in Prayer

Therefore if any man be in Christ, he is a new creature; old things are passed away; behold, all things are become new.

—2 CORINTHIANS 5:17

BUT THE SECRET *of Christianity is not in doing. The secret is in being. Real Christianity is in being a possessor of the nature of Jesus Christ. In other words, it is being Christ in character, Christ in demonstration, and Christ in agency of transmission. When one gives himself to the Lord and becomes a child of God, all that he does and all that he says from that time on should be the will, the words, and the actions of Jesus, just as absolutely and as entirely as Jesus spoke and did the will of the Father.*

What are you trying to do for God? If it's you trying, then stop trying and start trusting. If what you are doing for God is in your own strength, then nothing will happen. If what you are doing for God is rooted in His strength, will, and love, then your prayers will move mountains.

On the following pie chart, different sections are labeled with specific areas of life. Shade each area to the degree it is totally surrendered to Christ and not lived in your own strength.

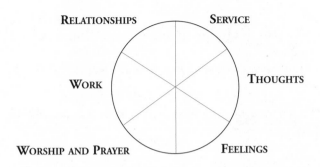

℘ESUS SHOWED US *that the only way to live this life was to commit oneself, as He did, to the will of God. He did not walk in His own ways at all, but walked in God's ways. So the one who is going to be a Christian in the best sense and let the world see Jesus in him must walk in all the ways of Jesus by following Him. He must be a Christ-man or Christ-woman—a Christian, or Christ-one.*

Surrendering to God's will is not a process of *doing* but of *being,* not a matter of *trying* but of *trusting,* and not an act of *achieving* but of *receiving.* Put yourself on the line in each of these areas of spiritual growth with an *x.*

In maturing as a Christian, I am . . .

Trusting   Still trying

Being   Doing

Receiving grace   Achieving

Ask Yourself . . .

❖ Who are you trying to impress with your faith and prayers?

❖ Are you working for God, or is He working through you?

Write a prayer confessing your need to be a new creation in Christ Jesus:

_____

_____

_____

Day 14

Trusting Totally

And he that taketh not his cross, and followeth after me,
is not worthy of me. He that findeth his life shall lose it:
and he that loseth his life for my sake shall find it.
                                        —MATTHEW 10:38–39

THE IMPRESSION I *wish to leave is this, that a hundredfold conse-*
cration to God takes the individual forever out of the hands of all
but God. This absolute consecration to God, this triune salva-
tion, is the real secret of the successful Christian life.

When one trusts any department of his being to man, he is weak in
that part of his being—not committed to God. When we trust our
minds (souls) and our bodies to man, two parts are out of the hands
of God, and what remains is simply our spirits in tune with heaven. It
ought not to be so. The committing of the whole being to the will of
God is the mind of God. Blessed be His name.

In prayer, one commits his whole being to Christ.
Nothing is held back. All is surrendered.

In the graphs below, indicate how surrendered each
area of your life is to Christ:

My prayer life:
/ / / / / / / / / /
Selfish   Surrendered

My family:
/ / / / / / / / / /
Selfish   Surrendered

My career: / / / / / / / / / /
Selfish   Surrendered

My will: / / / / / / / / / /
Selfish   Surrendered

My thoughts: / / / / / / / / / /
Selfish   Surrendered

My emotions: / / / / / / / / / /
Selfish   Surrendered

---

*S*UCH A COMMITMENT *of the being to God puts one in the place where, just as God supplies health to the spirit and health to the soul, he also trusts God to supply health to his body. Divine healing is the removal by the power of God of the disease that has come upon the body, but divine health is to live day by day and hour by hour in touch with God so that the life of God flows into the body, just as the life of God flows into the mind or flows into the spirit.*

His health overcomes my disease, robbing disease of all power and authority in my body. At the cross we exchange all we have and are for all He has and is. For example, I exchange my death for His life, my disease for His health. Write down other exchanges you may think of:

I exchange my . . .   **For His . . .**

_____   _____
_____   _____
_____   _____
_____   _____
_____   _____

Read Isaiah 53, and then add to the list above anything you may not have included on it.

Ask Yourself . . .

❖ Are you totally committed to Christ?
❖ Is the exchange with Him at the cross complete?

Write a prayer thanking Christ for what He did for you on the cross:

_____

_____

_____

Day 15

Shut Out Evil

Behold, I [Jesus] give unto you power to tread on serpents and scorpions, and over all the power of the enemy: and nothing shall by any means hurt you.

—LUKE 10:19

I TELL YOU, beloved, it is not necessary for people to be dominated by evil, nor by evil spirits. Instead of being dominated, Christians should exercise dominion, and control other forces. Even Satan has no power over them, only as they permit him to have. Jesus taught us to close the mind, to close the heart, to close the being against all that is evil and to live with an openness to God only, so that the sunlight and glory-radiance of God shines in and shuts out everything that is dark.

In prayer, are you willing to shut the door to every evil that tempts and attacks you? Check those things below that you need to shut the door to in your life:

❏ Lust
❏ Greed
❏ Gossip
❏ Anger
❏ Pornography
❏ Fear
❏ Dishonoring parents
❏ Substance abuse
❏ Pride

❏ Materialism
❏ Workaholism
❏ Laziness
❏ Immorality
❏ Bitterness
❏ Idolatry
❏ Unbelief
❏ The occult
❏ Other:

ESUS SAID, *"Take heed therefore how ye hear"* (Luke 8:18) — not
what you hear. One cannot help what he hears, but he can take
heed how he hears. When it is something offensive to the Spirit
and to the knowledge of God, shut the doors against it, and it will not
touch you.

The Christian lives as God wills in the world, dominating sin, evil,
and sickness. I would to God that He would be lifted up until all
believers would realize their privilege in Christ Jesus.

By the Spirit within us we cast out or expel from our beings all that
is not God-like. If you find within your heart a thought of sin or selfishness, by the exercise of the Spirit of God within you, cast that thing
out as unworthy of a child of God, and put it away from you. God
says to us, *"Be ye holy; for I am holy"* (1 Pet. 1:16).

What is the source of attack and unholiness in your
life? Are you willing to do away with it? Rank those
things that bring profanity into your life, and then commit yourself to guarding your ears and hearts from them:
(Rank from 1—the *most* tempting and profane, to 7—
the *least* tempting and profane.)

_____ Television

_____ Movies and videos

_____ Magazines

_____ Newspapers

_____ The talk of

_____ Radio

_____ Other:

Ask Yourself . . .

❖ Are you willing to purify yourself?
❖ What doors to sin are open in your life that need to be shut?

Ask the Lord to shut those doors:

_____

_____

_____

Day 16

Practicing His Presence in Prayer

Pray without ceasing.

—1 THESSALONIANS 5:17

SOME MAY HAVE *read the booklet by Brother Lawrence,* *"Practicing the Presence of Christ." It speaks of a necessity in the* *Christian life—His presence that is always with us.*

One of the things the Christian world does not get hold of with a *strong grip is the conscious presence of Christ with us now. Somehow* *there is an inclination in the Christian spirit to feel that Jesus, when* *He left the earth and returned to glory, is not present with us now.*

I want to show you how wonderfully the Scriptures emphasize the *fact of His presence with us now. His promise, after the great* *commission to the eleven disciples, was, "I am with you always."*

You can pray anytime, anyplace, and about anything. You can pray without ceasing. How? You live always mindful of God's presence, His Spirit, within and around you. Every conversation, action, feeling, and thought is Spirit-led. You can pray anyplace. Underline all the places you usually pray, and circle all the places you can begin praying:

In the shower

Working

Cleaning the house

Relaxing

First thing in the morning

Driving the car

Mowing the yard

Cooking a meal

Reading

Last thing at night

IT WOULD NATURALLY *seem as if a separation had been contemplated because of His return to glory, but no such separation is contemplated on the part of Christ. Christ promises His omnipotent presence with us always. Christ is everywhere and thus omnipresent—present in the soul, present in the world, and present unto the end of the age.*

Christ is the living presence of God, not only with us, but to the real Christian. He is in us as the perpetual joy, power, and glory of God. When a soul reaches to the heights of God, it will only be because of the guiding, counseling, indwelling, and infilling of the Christ.

To pray without ceasing is to practice God's presence constantly—anytime, anyplace, and with any kind of prayer. Begin your day by praying in His presence. Read these passages, and discover how to start each day in His presence:

Psalm 46:4–5 _____

_____

Psalm 63:1 _____

_____

Psalm 90:14 _____

_____

Proverbs 1:28; 8:17 _____

_____

Lamentations 3:22–24 _____

_____

Day 16

Ask Yourself . . .

❖ Are you seeking God's presence in prayer all the time and in all places?
❖ Are you starting off early each day in His presence?

Write a prayer asking God's Spirit to inspire you to pray without ceasing:

_____

_____

_____

Day 17

Knowing God

*Thou wilt keep him in perfect peace, whose mind is
stayed on thee.*

—ISAIAH 26:3

HERE IS A *quickening by the Spirit of God so that one's body,
soul or mind, and spirit all alike may become blessed, pervaded,
and filled with the presence of God Himself. The Word of God
is wonderfully clear along these lines. For instance, the Word of God
asserts, "Thou wilt keep him in perfect peace, whose mind is stayed on
thee" (Isa. 26:3). Why? "Because he trusteth in thee." That is the rest
that a Christian knows whose mind has perfect trust in God.*

In prayer, we are still before God. We silence every
voice so that His gentle whisper can be heard (1 Kings
19). He will compete with no other voice in our lives.
Only when we silence all idols and center entirely on
Him does He speak to our lives. Read these verses about
being still and waiting upon Him. Write down what they
reveal to you.

1 Kings 19:12 _____

_____

Psalm 37:7 _____

_____

Psalm 46:10 _____

_____

Psalm 62:1 _____

_____

Isaiah 40:31 _____

_____

1 Thessalonians 5:6 _____

_____

1 Peter 4:7 _____

_____

HE WORD OF God *says that our hearts will rejoice, and our flesh will rest in hope (Ps. 16:9). Not our mind, but our very flesh shall hope and rest in God. God is to be a living presence, not only in the spirit of man, nor in the mind of man alone, but also in the flesh of man, so that God is known in all departments of life. We know God in our very flesh. We know God in our mind. We know God in our spirit.*

To know God is to have an intimate, personal relationship with Him. He knows us intimately. Read Psalm 139, and list all the ways that He knows us:

_____

_____

_____

We know God through hours, days, weeks, and months of prayer. As we pray, we come to know His voice, His will, and His way. Communion with Him reveals His nature to us. Complete the following sentences:

Through prayer, I know that God is _____

_____ .

I listen best to God's voice when I _____

_____ .

Waiting on God has taught me _____

_____ .

Ask Yourself . . .

❖ Am I waiting on the Lord or trying to force things to go my way?
❖ Do I desire an intimate relationship with God or just want my needs to be met by Him?

Spend thirty minutes in silence, waiting for God's voice. Meditate on Psalm 46:10 and Isaiah 40:31.

_____

_____

_____

Day 18

Prayer and Ministry

I will pray with the spirit, and I will pray with the understanding also: I will sing with the spirit, and I will sing with the understanding also.
                                        —1 Corinthians 14:15

THE MINISTRY OF *the Christian is the ministry of the Spirit. If the Christian cannot minister the Spirit of God, in the true sense he is not a Christian. If he has not the Spirit to minister, in the highest sense he has nothing to minister. Other men have intellectual knowledge, but the Christian is supposed to be the possessor of the Spirit.*

Ministry begins in prayer. Without prayer nothing happens. We pray and sing in the spirit so that the gifts within us may be stirred up and released for others.

Read 1 Timothy 1:6–7. In your own words describe what Paul tells Timothy about the ministry gift that he has:

_____

_____

The Holy Spirit has inspired within you mighty gifts for ministry that can only be released through prayer. Through prayer the Spirit communicates God's will for ministry and releases power to use His gifts. What are those gifts released by prayer? Read the following scriptures, and list on the gift pictured below all the gifts you find (Rom. 12:5–8; 1 Cor. 12; Eph. 4:7–16; 1 Pet. 4:10–11).

Look over the list that you have just written. Circle all the gifts that you have used in ministry. Underline every gift that has been ministered to you. The church is built up as we minister to one another and pray in the Spirit.

Read Jude 20, and then rewrite it in your own words:

Ask Yourself . . .

* Are you praying in the Spirit, seeking the ministry He would have for you to do?
* What gifts does the Spirit desire for you to use in ministering to the body?

Write a prayer asking God to reveal to you the gifts He desires to stir up within you:

Day 19

Hungering for God

Blessed are they which do hunger and thirst after
righteousness: for they shall be filled.
—MATTHEW 5:6

UNGER IS A *mighty good thing. It is the greatest persuader I*
know. It is a marvelous mover. Nations have learned that you
can do almost anything with a populace until they get hungry.
But when they get hungry you want to watch out. There is a certain
spirit of desperation that accompanies hunger.

I wish we all had such desperate spiritual hunger. I wish to God we
were desperately hungry for God. Wouldn't it be glorious? It would be
a strange thing if we were all desperately hungry for God, but only one
or two individuals got filled in a service. If everyone in a service was
desperately hungry for God, how much more the whole assembly
would experience the filling of the Holy Spirit.

"Blessed are they which do hunger and thirst after righteousness."
Righteousness is "the rightness of God"—the rightness of God in
your spirit, the rightness of God in your soul, the rightness of God in
your body, and the rightness of God in your affairs, home, business,
and in every aspect of your life.

The more you pray, the greater your hunger for God
will be. Prayer doesn't satisfy your hunger for Him. Only
His presence satisfies your hungering and thirsting after
His righteousness. But prayer increases your desire to be
more and more in His presence.

How much are you hungering and thirsting after His righteousness? Put an *x* on the line where you are now:

My hunger for Him is

_____

Increasing   Decreasing

My time with Him in prayer is

_____

Increasing   Decreasing

My desire for His presence is

_____

Increasing   Decreasing

OD IS AN *all-round God. His power operates from every side. There is a radiation of glory from His person. It is the radiant glory of the indwelling God, radiating out through the personality. There is nothing more wonderful than the indwelling of God in the human life. The most supreme marvel that God ever performed was when He took possession of those who are hungry for righteousness, and filled them!*

Read Psalm 42:1–2. Complete these sentences:

The Lord satisfies my thirst when _____

_____ .

I am closest to the Lord when _____

_____ .

Day 19

Ask Yourself . . .

❖ Are you hungering intensely for His righteousness?
❖ Is He taking possession of you?

Write a prayer of hunger for His righteousness:

_____

_____

_____

Day 20

Praying the Cross

*But God forbid that I should glory, save in the cross of
our Lord Jesus Christ, by whom the world is crucified
unto me, and I unto the world.*

—GALATIANS 6:14

MEN HAVE SAID *that the cross of Christ was not a heroic thing, but
I want to tell you that the cross of Jesus Christ has put more
heroism in the souls of men than any other event in human history. Men have lived, rejoiced, and died believing in the living God, in
the Christ of God whose blood cleansed their hearts from sin, and who
have realized the real high spirit of His holy sacrifice, bless God.*

Praying the cross begins with *repentance*—turning
away from sin and the world and to Jesus Christ. Read
the following passages, and write down what they say
about repentance:

Matthew 4:17

Acts 2:38

Acts 3:19

2 Corinthians 7:10 _____

_____

    Praying the cross inspires *confession*—agreeing with God that we are sinners and need the Savior, Jesus Christ. Write down what each of the following verses say about confession:

Matthew 10:32 _____

_____

Romans 10:9 _____

_____

Philippians 2:11 _____

_____

1 John 1:8 _____

_____

> HEY MANIFESTED TO *mankind that same measure of sacrifice, and endured all that human beings could endure. When endurance was no longer possible, they passed on to be with God, leaving the world blessed through the evidence of a consecration deep and true and pure and good, like the Son of God Himself.*

    Praying the cross demands *sacrifice*—offering ourselves totally in surrender to Christ. Read the following verses, and write down what the Bible says about sacrifice:

Psalm 51:16–17

Romans 12:1–2

Galatians 2:20

Ask Yourself . . .

❖ Are you needing to repent or confess?
❖ What sacrifice is the Lord asking you to make?

Write a prayer asking the Lord to make your life a living sacrifice:

Day 21

The Higher Life

And hath raised us up together, and made us sit together in heavenly places in Christ Jesus.

—EPHESIANS 2:6

ELOVED, THAT IS *the difficulty with us all. We have come down out of the heavenlies into the natural, and we are trying to live a heavenly life in the natural state, overburdened by the weights and cares of the flesh and life all about us. Bless God, there is deliverance. There is victory. There is a place in God where the flesh no longer becomes a bondage. Where, by the grace of God, every sensuous state of the human nature is brought into subjection to the living God, where Christ reigns in and glorifies the very activities of a man's nature, making him sweet and pure and clean and good and true.*

Prayer focuses our beings on the spiritual and heavenly things of life. No longer are we centered on the flesh and the things of the flesh. The Spirit praying through us directs our attention to the fruit of the Spirit.

Read Galatians 5:22–26. On the following page is a group of fruit with one fruit of the Spirit listed on each piece of fruit. Circle the name of each fruit that needs to mature in your life through prayer, and underline each fruit that has been manifested recently in your life as you have prayed in the Spirit.

I CALL YOU *today, Beloved, by the grace of God, to that higher life, to that holy walk, to that heavenly atmosphere, to that life in God where the grace and Spirit and power of God permeate your whole being. Where not only your whole being is in subjection, but God's Spirit flows from your nature as a holy stream of heavenly life to bless other souls everywhere by the grace of God.*

Prayer opens the floodgates to the river of God flowing from His throne into your life. Read John 7:38–39 and Revelation 22:1–3. Check all the aspects of God's river that you need to have flowing through your life as you pray:

- ❏ Cleansing
- ❏ Refreshing
- ❏ Renewing
- ❏ Reviving
- ❏ Baptizing
- ❏ Washing
- ❏ Replenishing

Ask Yourself . . .

❖ Is your prayer life focused on the heavenlies or only on natural things?

❖ How is the river of God flowing through you as you pray?

Write a prayer for the river of God to flow through you:

_____

_____

_____

Day 22

Repent of Denying God's Power

For I am not ashamed of the gospel of Christ: for it is the power of God unto salvation to every one that believeth; to the Jew first, and also to the Greek.

— ROMANS 1:16

IN EVERY LAND, *among every people, throughout all history, there have been occasions when a demonstration of the power of God was just as necessary to the world as it was in the days of Elijah (1 Kings 18:17–40). It is necessary now.*

The people in Elijah's day had turned away from God. They had forgotten that there was a God in Israel. They were trusting in other gods, just as people are today. If I were to call you heathen, I suppose most people would be offended.

Idolatry destroys prayer. Idolatry in our nation makes the heavens as brass. What are some of the idols that need to be destroyed in our nation? Rank from the *most* (1), to the *least* threatening (7) the idols that attack our land:

_____ Materialism

_____ Drug abuse

_____ Crime

_____ Greed

_____ Lying and deception
_____ Rebellion
_____ Witchcraft and the occult
_____ Abuse
_____ Immorality
_____ Other: _____

THERE ARE NO people with more gods than the average American. Men are bowing down to the god of medicine. Men are bowing down to the god of popularity. Men are as afraid of the opinion of their neighbors as any heathen ever was in any time in the world. There is practically no Christian who has the stamina to stand forth and declare his absolute convictions concerning Jesus Christ, the Son of God. Much less have men the necessary stamina to declare their convictions as to Jesus Christ, the Savior of mankind.

That is the reason that the modern church has lost her touch with God and has gone into a sleep unto death, a sleep that can only end in spiritual death and the disintegration of the church as she stands. The only power that will revive the church in this world is that which she will receive when she throws her heart open to God as the people of Israel did and says, "Lord God, we have sinned." The sin she needs to repent of is not the committing of a lot of little acts which men call sin. These are the outgrowth of what is in the heart. The thing that mankind needs to repent of is this: That they have denied the power of God.

Read 2 Chronicles 7:14, and then write a prayer based on that verse that will be a prayer of repentance for our nation:

_____

_____

_____

Ask Yourself . . .

❖ What sins do you need to repent of?
❖ Are you praying daily for your nation's salvation?

Read aloud the prayer of repentance that you have just written.

_____

_____

_____

Day 23

Christ Living in You

I am crucified with Christ: nevertheless I live; yet not I, but Christ liveth in me.

—GALATIANS 2:20

T HAT IS THE *text: "Christ liveth in me." That is the revelation of this age. That is the discovery of the moment. That is the revolutionizing power of God in the earth. It is the factor that is changing the spirit of religion in the world and the character of Christian faith. It is divine vitalization. The world is awakening to that marvelous truth, that Christ is not in the heavens only, nor in the atmosphere only, but Christ is in you.*

Christ living in you through His Spirit empowers you to pray. Read Romans 8:26–27. Rewrite that passage in your own words:

_____

_____

_____

The world lived in darkness for thousands of years. There was just as much electricity in the world then as now. It is not that electricity has just come into being. It was always here. But men have discovered how to utilize it and bless themselves with it.

Christ's indwelling in the human heart is the mystery of mysteries. Paul gave it to the Gentiles as the supreme mystery of all the revelation of God and the finality of all wonder He knew. "Christ in you."

Christ has a purpose in you. Christ's purpose is to reveal Himself to you, through you, and in you.

Ask Yourself . . .

❖ Are you fulfilling Christ's purpose in your life?
❖ Do others see Christ in you?

Write a prayer thanking Christ for indwelling you:

_____

_____

_____

Day 24

Prayer and Love

Now abideth faith, hope, charity, these three; but the greatest of these is charity [love].
—1 CORINTHIANS 13:13

HERE IS ONE *great thing that the world is needing more than anything else, and I am convinced of it every day I live. Humanity has one supreme need, and that is the love of God. The hearts of men are dying for lack of the love of God.*

Pray that the Lord gives you His love (*agape*) for others. God's love is unconditional acceptance—it wants His best for the other person. Pray for His love as described in 1 Corinthians 13. Complete the sentences below, based on 1 Corinthians 13.

Lord, grant me patience to _____ .

Lord, make me kind toward _____ .

Lord, help me not to envy _____ .

Lord, take away my pride that _____ .

Lord, help me not to be rude when _____ .

Lord, remove my selfishness for _____ .

Lord, keep me from being provoked when _____.

Lord, keep me from thinking evil about _____.

Lord, fill me with joy for _____.

Lord, grant me endurance, hope, and strength for _____.

I HAVE A *sister in Detroit. She came over to Milwaukee to visit us for two or three days at the convention there. As I watched her moving around, I thought, I would like to take her along and just have her love folks. She would not need to preach. You do not need to preach to folks. It is not the words you say that are going to bless them. They need something greater. It is the thing in your soul. They have to receive it, then their soul will open and there will be a divine response. Give it to them, it is the love of God.*

You have seen people who loved someone who would not respond. If there is any hard situation in God's earth, that is it, to passionately love someone and find no response in them.

Read Matthew 22:39 and 1 John 4:11–18. For whom do you need to pray and show God's love in all that you say and do? Make a list.

People to love and pray for . . .

A friend _____

An enemy _____

A favorite family member _____

A family member who is hard to love _____

Someone at church _____

Someone at work _____

A stranger _____

A town or nation _____

Simply loving those who love us does not fulfill God's command to love. Pray for and love your enemies (Matt. 5:43–48).

Ask Yourself . . .

❖ Are you loving your enemies?
❖ How are you showing Christ's love to others?

Write a prayer asking God to give you His love for others:

_____

_____

_____

Day 25

Let Go of Others

Be kindly affectioned one to another with brotherly love; in honor preferring one another.

—ROMANS 12:10

D O NOT HOLD *people. Do not bind people. Just cut them loose, and let God love them. Don't you know we hold people with such a grip when we pray for them that they miss the blessing? Why, you have such a grip on your humanity that it is exercising itself, and the spirit is being submerged. Let your soul relax, and let the Spirit of God in you find vent. There is no substitute for the love of God. "Christ in you" (Col. 1:27). Oh, you have the capacity to love. All the action of the Spirit of God has its secret there.*

Through prayer, Christ in you reveals the acts of kindness He would have you do for others. Make a list below of people you are praying for and the acts of kindness God would have you do in their lives:

Name   **Act of Kindness**

_____   _____

_____   _____

_____   _____

_____   _____

_____   _____

STOOD ON ONE *occasion by a dying woman who was suffering and writhing in awful agony. I had prayed again and again with no results. But this day something happened inside me. My soul broke down, and I saw that poor soul in a new light. Before, I knew it I reached out and gathered her in my arms and hugged her up to my soul, not my bosom.*

In a minute I knew the real thing had taken place. I laid her back down on the pillow. In five minutes she was well. God was waiting until He could get to my soul with the sense of the tenderness that was in the Son of God.

God desires to inspire in you the same compassion and comfort that Christ had in His ministry. That comfort is described in 2 Corinthians 1:1–11. Read this passage, and then complete these thoughts:

The one who comforts us in all our tribulations is ____

_____.

One reason He comforts us is so that we _____

_____.

One thing that abounds in us is _____

_____.

We can be certain that _____

_____.

Dare we pray to comfort others to the degree that we bear His sufferings in our bodies? Paul writes, "That I may know him, and the power of his resurrection, and the fellowship of his sufferings, being made conformable

unto his death" (Phil. 3:10–11). Mother Teresa identi-
fied with the sufferings of children and lepers in India.
Dare we pray for such fellowship with His sufferings?
What would hinder such a prayer in you? Circle all that
would hinder:

Fear
Too busy
Lack of compassion
Unbelief
Other: _____

Ask Yourself . . .

❖ Are you willing to pray that God will use you to
   comfort others?
❖ Will you fellowship with His sufferings?

*Write a prayer seeking to know Christ through the fellowship
of His sufferings:*

_____

_____

_____

Day 26

The Development of the Soul

That I may know him, and the power of his resurrection, and the fellowship of his sufferings.
—PHILIPPIANS 3:10

WE LIVE THAT *our souls may grow. The development of the soul is the purpose of existence. By His grace He is endeavoring to have us grow up in His knowledge and likeness to that stature where, as sons of God, we will comprehend something of His love, of His nature, of His power, of His purpose. Then we will be big enough to give back to God what a son should give to a great Father — the reverence, the love, the affection that comes from understanding the greatness of His purpose.*

Yesterday we began to explore how we know Christ through the fellowship of His sufferings. That knowledge begins in prayer and extends in ministry.

Read Matthew 25:31–46. Then complete the following:

Those for whom I am praying who are hungry are ____

_____ .

One way I am feeding the hungry is _____

_____ .

Those for whom I am praying who are thirsty are ____

_____ .

One way I am giving a cup of water in Jesus' name is

_____.

Those for whom I am praying who are strangers and homeless are _____.

One way I minister to the homeless and strangers is

_____.

The poor and naked for whom I pray are _____

_____.

One way I clothe the naked is _____

_____.

The sick for whom I pray are _____

_____.

One way I visit the sick is _____

_____.

Those in prison for whom I pray are _____

_____.

One way I minister to those in prison is _____

_____.

Ask Yourself . . .

❖ Do you pray before you minister?
❖ Do you minister to others after you pray?

Write a prayer for "the least of these:"

_____

_____

_____

Day 27

Holiness and Power

But ye shall receive power, after that the Holy Ghost is come upon you.

—ACTS 1:8

NOT LONG AGO *I stood before great audiences of the churchmen of the world. Someone said, "Do you not think it would be better if the church was calling for holiness instead of power?"*
And I replied, "She will never obtain the one without the other. There is something larger than holiness. It is the nature of God."

Consider the attributes of God. Take about fifteen minutes to skim through the Psalms, writting down as many attributes of God as you can find.

THE NATURE OF *God has many sides. From every angle that the soul approaches God, a new and different aspect of God is revealed: love, beauty, tenderness, healing, power, might, and wisdom.*
The Christian who hungers and lifts his soul to God, brings God down to meet his own cry. The spirit of man and the Spirit of God unite. The nature of God is reproduced in man.

The Spirit of God produces Christ's nature in us through the fruit of the Spirit. Read Galatians 5:22–26. Then pray through the fruit of the Spirit:

Christ, increase love in me _____ .

Christ, increase joy in me _____ .

Christ, increase peace in me _____ .

Christ, increase patience in me _____ .

Christ, increase gentleness in me _____ .

Christ, increase goodness in me _____ .

Christ, increase humility in me _____ .

Christ, increase self-control in me _____ .

Ask Yourself . . .

❖ Is your nature conforming more and more to His nature?
❖ Do others see Christ in you?

Write a prayer asking for Christ to increase and for you to decrease in your life.

_____

_____

_____

Day 28

Christ's Fullness in Us

Till we all come in the unity of the faith, and of the knowledge of the Son of God, unto a perfect man, unto the measure of the stature of the fullness of Christ.
— EPHESIANS 4:13

EXPERIMENTALLY I KNEW *God as Savior from sin, I knew the power of the Christ within my own heart to keep me above the power of temptation and to help me live a godly life. But when the purpose of God in the salvation of man first dawned upon my soul, that is, when the greatness of it dawned upon my soul, life became for me a grand, new thing.*

By the study of God's Word, and by the revelation of His Spirit, it became a fact in my soul that God's purpose was no less in me than it was in the Lord Jesus. His purpose is no less in you and I, as younger brethren, than it was in Jesus Christ, our elder brother. Then I saw the purpose that God had in mind for the human race. Then I saw the greatness of Jesus' desire. That desire that was so intense it caused Him, as King of Glory, to lay down all that glory possessed for Him, and come to earth to be born as a man. He joined hands with our humanity, and by His grace lifts us in consciousness and life to the same level that He Himself enjoyed. Christ became a new factor in my soul. A vision of His purpose thrilled my being. I could understand then how Jesus approached man and his needs at the very bottom, calling mankind to Him. Then by His loving touch and the power of the Spirit through His word, He destroyed the sickness and sin that bound man and set us free both in body and in soul.

You have read Lake's testimony; now write yours. What has Jesus Christ done in your life? How has He become your Lord and Savior?

∼◌◌◌∼

_____

_____

_____

_____

_____

_____

_____

_____

_____

Ask Yourself . . .

❖ With whom will I share my testimony today?
❖ How will my relationship with Christ deepen today?

Write a prayer thanking Jesus for saving you:

_____

_____

_____

Day 29

Total Commitment

And the very God of peace sanctify you wholly; and I pray God your whole spirit and soul and body be preserved blameless unto the coming of our Lord Jesus Christ.

—1 THESSALONIANS 5:23

FIRST COMMIT *your body and soul and spirit in entire, hundred-fold consecration to God forever. Do not be satisfied with sins forgiven.*

Lord Jesus, I commit . . .

_____

_____

_____ .

PRESS ON, *press in, let God have you and fill you, until consciously He dwells, lives, abides in every cell of your blood, your bone, and your brain; until your soul, indwelt by Him, thinks His thoughts, speaks His Word; until your spirit assimilates God, and God's Spirit assimilates you; until your humanity and His divinity are merged into His eternal Deity. Thus body, soul, and spirit are God's forever.*

God, fill me with . . .

_____

_____ .

Spirit of God, help me to press on and in to . . .

_____

_____ .

Ask Yourself . . .

❖ Have I surrendered all to Christ?
❖ Am I holding back or pressing in to Him?

Write a prayer of total surrender to Christ:

_____

_____

_____

Day 30

Divine Healing

For I am the Lord that healeth thee.

—EXODUS 15:26

IN DIVINE HEALING *today, the unchangeableness of God's eternal purpose is thereby demonstrated. "Jesus Christ the same yesterday, and today and for ever" (Heb. 13:8). "I am the Lord, I change not" (Mal. 3:6).*

God always was the healer. He is the healer still, and will ever remain the healer. Healing is for you. Jesus healed all that came to Him. He never turned anyone away. He never said: "It is not God's will to heal you," or that it was better for the individual to remain sick, or that they were being perfected in character through the sickness.

Jesus healed them all, thereby demonstrating forever God's unchangeable will concerning sickness and healing. Have you need of healing? Pray to God in the name of Jesus Christ to remove the disease. Command it to leave you, as you would sin. Assert your divine authority, and refuse to have it. Jesus purchased your freedom from sickness as He purchased your freedom from sin.

Lord, I ask you to heal _____

_____.

81

Lord, I speak healing in the authority of the name of Jesus that I be healed from _____

_____ .

I refuse, in Jesus' name, to be sick from _____

_____ .

I declare my freedom from _____ in Jesus' name.

Take a few moments to reflect on what has been revealed to you in this study. Complete these sentences:

My prayer life has grown in _____

_____ .

I have discovered that prayer is _____

_____ .

I am now praying for _____

_____ .

One way I am closer to Christ is _____

_____ .

One way I have been changed by the Holy Spirit in this devotional study is _____

_____ .

Ask Yourself . . .

❖ Are you willing to pray and live boldly for Christ?
❖ Will you continue to grow in your prayer life?

Write a prayer thanking the Lord for the privilege of prayer:

_____

_____

_____

Leader's Guide

For Group Sessions

This devotional study is an excellent resource for group study including such settings as:

- ❖ Sunday school classes and other church classes.
- ❖ Prayer groups.
- ❖ Bible study groups.
- ❖ Ministries involving small groups, home groups, and accountability groups.
- ❖ Study groups for youth and adults.

Before the first session

- ❖ Contact everyone interested or already participating in the group about the meeting time, date, and place.
- ❖ Make certain that everyone has a copy of this devotional study guide, *The Original John G. Lake Devotional*, and the *Holy Spirit Encounter Bible*.
- ❖ Ask group members to begin their daily encounters in this guide. Plan for six sessions with each group session covering five devotional studies. Group members who faithfully do a devotional each day will be prepared to share in the group sessions. Plan out all your sessions before starting the first session.
- ❖ Pray for the Holy Spirit to guide, teach, and help each participant.
- ❖ Be certain that the place where you will meet has a chalkboard, white board, or flip chart with

appropriate writing materials. It is also best to be in a setting with movable, not fixed, seating.

Planning the Group Sessions

1. You will have six sessions together as a group. Plan to cover at least five days in each session.

2. In your first session, allow group members to select a partner with whom they will share and pray during each session. Keep the same pairs throughout the group sessions. You can put pairs together randomly—men with men and women with women.

3. Begin each session with prayer.

4. Read or ask group members to read the key scriptures at the start of each daily devotional for the five days prior to that session.

5. Prior to each session, decide which exercises and questions you would like to cover from the five daily devotional studies for that session.

6. Decide which exercises and sessions will be most appropriate for your group to share as a whole and which would be more comfortable for group members to share in pairs.

7. From the five previous days, decide which prayer(s) you wish the pairs to pray with one another.

8. Close each session with each group member sharing with the total group how he or she grew in faith during the previous week. Then lead the group in prayer or have group members pray aloud. Close the session with your own prayer.

9. In the last session, use the thirtieth day as an in-depth sharing time in pairs. Invite all the

group members to share the most important thing they learned about prayer during this study and how their relationship with the Lord was deepened during the study. Close with prayers of praise and thanksgiving.

10. Whether sharing in pairs or as a total group, remember to allow each person the freedom not to share if they are not comfortable.

11. Be careful. This is not a therapy group. Group members who seek to dominate group discussions with their own problems or questions should be ministered to by the group leader or pastor in a one-on-one setting outside of the group session.

12. Always start and end the group session on time, and seek to keep the session within a ninety-minute time frame.